THE RISING

At Easter 1916, while England fought a war in Europe and the Middle East, Irish rebels struck a blow for their independence. The flag of the Irish Republic was raised on the roof of their HQ at the General Post Office.

Pádraig Pearse read the Proclamation of the Irish Republic, declaring all the people of Ireland equal citizens of their own independent state.

EVERYBODY OUT.

The Rebels took over the G.P.O. The Rising had begun.

EASTER RISING

MICHAEL COLLINS
IRELAND'S REBEL SON

DAVID BUTLER   **MARIO CORRIGAN**

LETTERING BY **FIONA BONIWELL**

THE O'BRIEN PRESS
DUBLIN

Dedications

DB – For John Butler my grandfather, a civilian in the Cav. Workshop on the Curragh, the only man allowed to weld the Sliabh na mBan. To Marcella, Erin, Ava & Kian for the support.

MC – For Eve, Jack and Rachel Corrigan, and their cousin Maren, whose beautiful spirit watches over us.

FB – To Matt and Phoenix, thanks for all of your love and support.

Originally from Kildare, animator and illustrator David Butler now lives in Portarlington, County Laois. He is a graduate of the Dun Laoghaire Film Institute of Ireland, Animation Production Course. He has worked on several award-winning projects, including the BAFTA award-winning 'Sir Gawain and the Green Knight'. David has illustrated four original children's books with Mario.
Website: anithing.ie
Instagram: @anithingartist · Twitter: @anithingartist

A librarian with Kildare Library Services, Mario Corrigan has written and edited many books on the history of Kildare. He has written four children's books with schoolchildren, all of which were illustrated by David Butler. As part of the Decade of Centenaries project in Kildare, he wrote a play A Terrible Beauty Exposed! and a narration for a series of concerts, Birth of a Nation, which included a performance in Lexington, Kentucky, USA. On 9 July 2022, he delivered the oration at the centenary commemoration for Cathal Brugha in Glasnevin Cemetery.
Website: mariocorriganblog.wordpress.com · Twitter: @mariomcorrigan

Fiona Boniwell is a comic creator based in Cork, Ireland. She has contributed to a number of Irish comics as an illustrator and lettering artist. Fiona also facilitates workshops and is equally passionate about creating and teaching comic art projects.
Her interests beyond comics centre on family and practising Kuk Sool Won (Korean martial arts) with them.
Website: boniwellgraphics.com
Instagram: @Boniwell_Graphics · Twitter: @FionaBoniwell

As the British converged on the GPO the rebels made their way through the back lanes and terraces, with little chance of success or survival.

CRACK

HERE, BOYS, HELP ME.

THIS WILL GIVE US COVER.

PING

KLINK KLANK

PING

Finally, the commanders took the decision to surrender.

WE MUST PREVENT FURTHER BLOODSHED AND LOSS OF CIVILIAN LIFE.

Nurse Elizabeth O'Farrell carried word to the British. Notification was sent to all the garrisons in the city.

Pádraig Pearse surrendered to Brigadier General Lowe, British commander in the field.

The Easter Rising was over.

Eventually the rebels were brought to Richmond Barracks. G-men circled like hyenas, identifying the known leaders of the Rising.

HERE'S ONE OF THE RINGLEADERS.

JOSEPH PLUNKETT. *REBEL SCUM.*

MOVE IT, PADDY.

NO PLANTING YOUR SHAMROCK HERE.

Within days, the 'rebels' were despatched to English prisons.

READY AIM FIRE!!

Mick learned about the execution of the leaders, including his beloved Plunkett and Connolly, while in Stafford Jail.

He and the other internees pledged to finish the job they had started at Easter 1916.

Michael Collins would free Ireland or die trying.

Collins developed an intelligence network with links to Dublin Castle and to the infamous 'G Division' of plain clothes detectives in Brunswick St. He was in no doubt there would be an armed conflict. He would see them prepared.

Brunswick House

His friend and loyal servant Joe O'Reilly was an intelligence officer, while his cousin Nancy O'Brien worked in the G.P.O. decoding messages. Friends such as Ned Broy, Joe Kavanagh, David Neligan and James MacNamara worked in the police and in Dublin Castle.

WHAT HAVE YOU FOR ME TODAY THEN, NED?

WE HAVE TO STAY A STEP AHEAD.

Lily Mernin, who worked in Dublin Castle, was able to identify G Men on sight.

I DID ALWAYS PROMISE I'D GIVE YOU THE SHIRT OFF ME BACK ...

...THEY'LL PAY, TOM, I SWEAR IT.

NOTHING ADDITIONAL REMAINS TO BE SAID. THAT VOLLEY WHICH WE HAVE JUST HEARD IS THE **ONLY SPEECH** WHICH IT IS PROPER TO MAKE ABOVE THE GRAVE OF A DEAD FENIAN.

KRAAACK

On 25 September 1917, Thomas Ashe died after being force fed while on hunger strike; the first martyr since 1916. His body was waked at City Hall, laid out in a shirt given by Michael Collins and a Volunteer tunic given by Eamon de Valera. 30,000 people lined the streets to Glasnevin cemetery. Mick gave a simple but effective oration, every bit as powerful as that delivered by Pearse over O'Donovan Rossa.

FROM THE ASHES

De Valera became President of Sinn Féin and of the Irish Volunteers, while Collins was appointed Adjutant General and Director of Organisation of the Volunteers. He relished it, collecting statistics and creating an inventory of arms and ammunition.

The Volunteers would be reorganised - the old British-style 'companies' would now be replaced by 'flying columns' for a guerrilla war, and the old uniform would be replaced by a trench coat in the countryside.

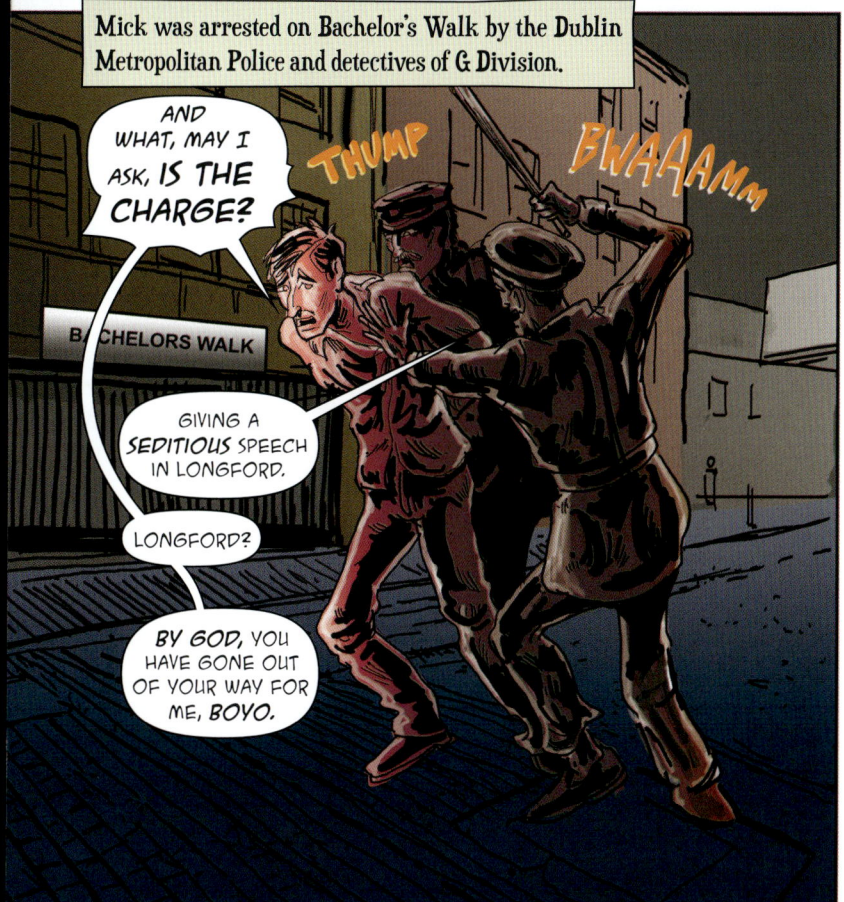

Mick was arrested on Bachelor's Walk by the Dublin Metropolitan Police and detectives of G Division.

AND WHAT, MAY I ASK, IS THE CHARGE?

THUMP
BWAAAMM

BACHELORS WALK

GIVING A SEDITIOUS SPEECH IN LONGFORD.

LONGFORD?

BY GOD, YOU HAVE GONE OUT OF YOUR WAY FOR ME, BOYO.

Mick was imprisoned in Sligo Jail, but posted bail and was released.

It was his last time behind bars - for the next three years, he was on the run.

"OUR SINN FÉIN VICTORY SHOWS THE **NECESSITY** OF AN IRISH PARLIAMENT FOR THE IRISH PEOPLE."

CLAP CLAP CLAP HEAR HEAR HEAR

VOTE MICHAEL COLLINS NUMBER 1

VOTE MICHAEL COLLINS NUMBER 1

Michael Collins was elected as an MP for Cork South. But he and the other Sinn Féiners chose not to take their seats in Westminster; instead they would set up an Irish Parliament in Dublin.

"I HEREBY PLEDGE MYSELF TO WORK FOR THE ESTABLISHMENT OF AN INDEPENDENT IRISH REPUBLIC;

THAT I WILL ACCEPT NOTHING LESS THAN COMPLETE SEPARATION FROM ENGLAND IN SETTLEMENT OF IRELAND'S CLAIMS;

AND THAT I WILL ABSTAIN FROM ATTENDING THE ENGLISH PARLIAMENT."

PLOTS, PRISON BREAKS AND POLITICS

21 January 1919, Mansion House, Dáil Éireann

"ANY SIGN OF BOLAND OR COLLINS?"

"I BELIEVE THEY ARE VISITING AN OLD FRIEND."

Michael Collins had done much to establish the new national assembly, Dáil Éireann, which met for the first time on 21 January 1919 in Dublin's Mansion House. Collins was appointed Minister for Home Affairs. He was marked present on the roll but was otherwise engaged... in England!

LINCOLN PRISON BREAK

"I HOPE DEV DOESN'T BREAK HIS TEETH ON THAT CAKE!"

Mick and others had hatched a plan to free De Valera, Seán McGarry and Seán Milroy from Lincoln Prison. Several attempts to replicate and smuggle in keys failed, but a new master key was made in the jail and smuggled out. Collins, Harry Boland and Paddy O'Donoghue from Manchester arrived in darkness in a taxi.

"GOOD MAN, MICHAEL."

18

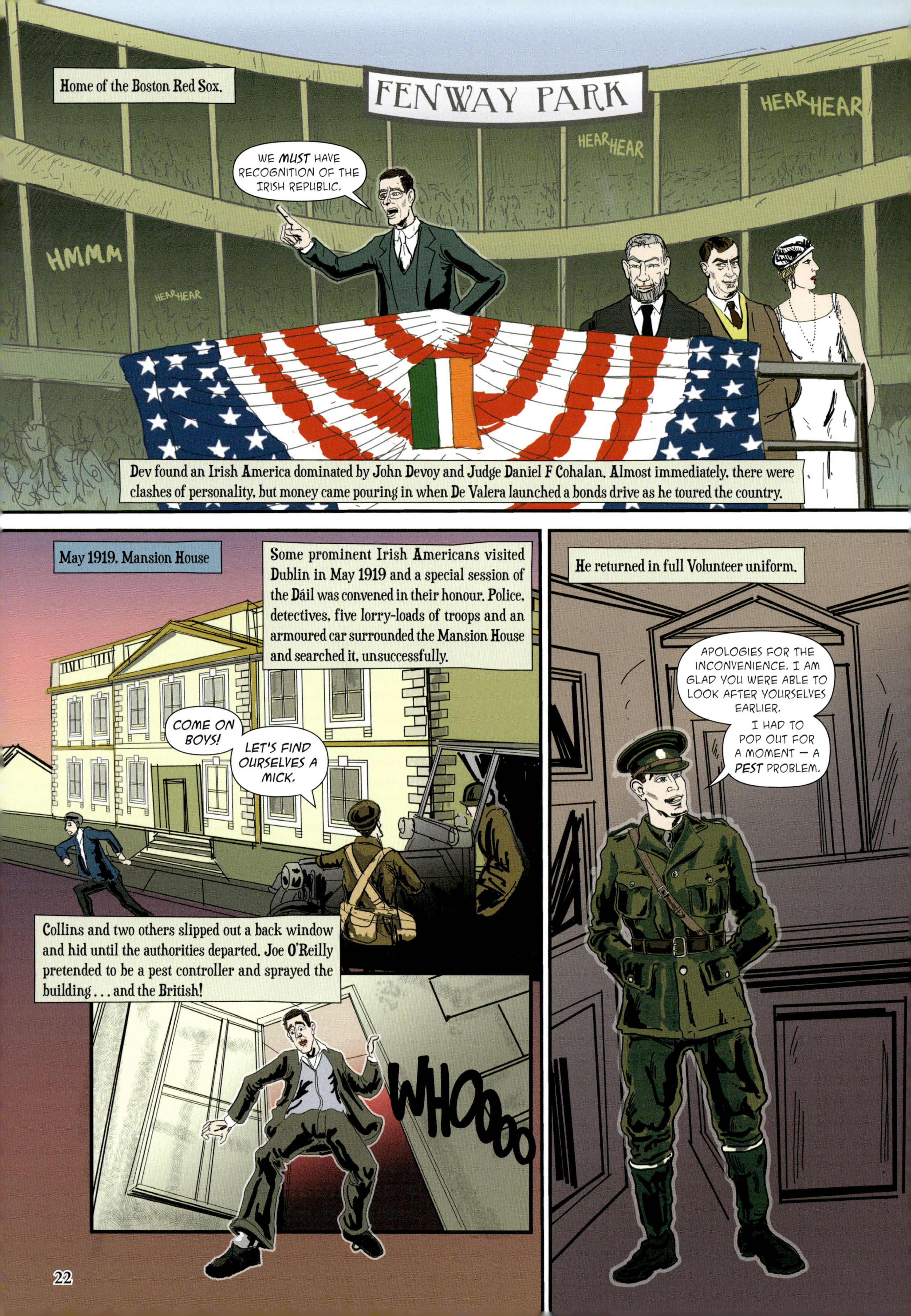

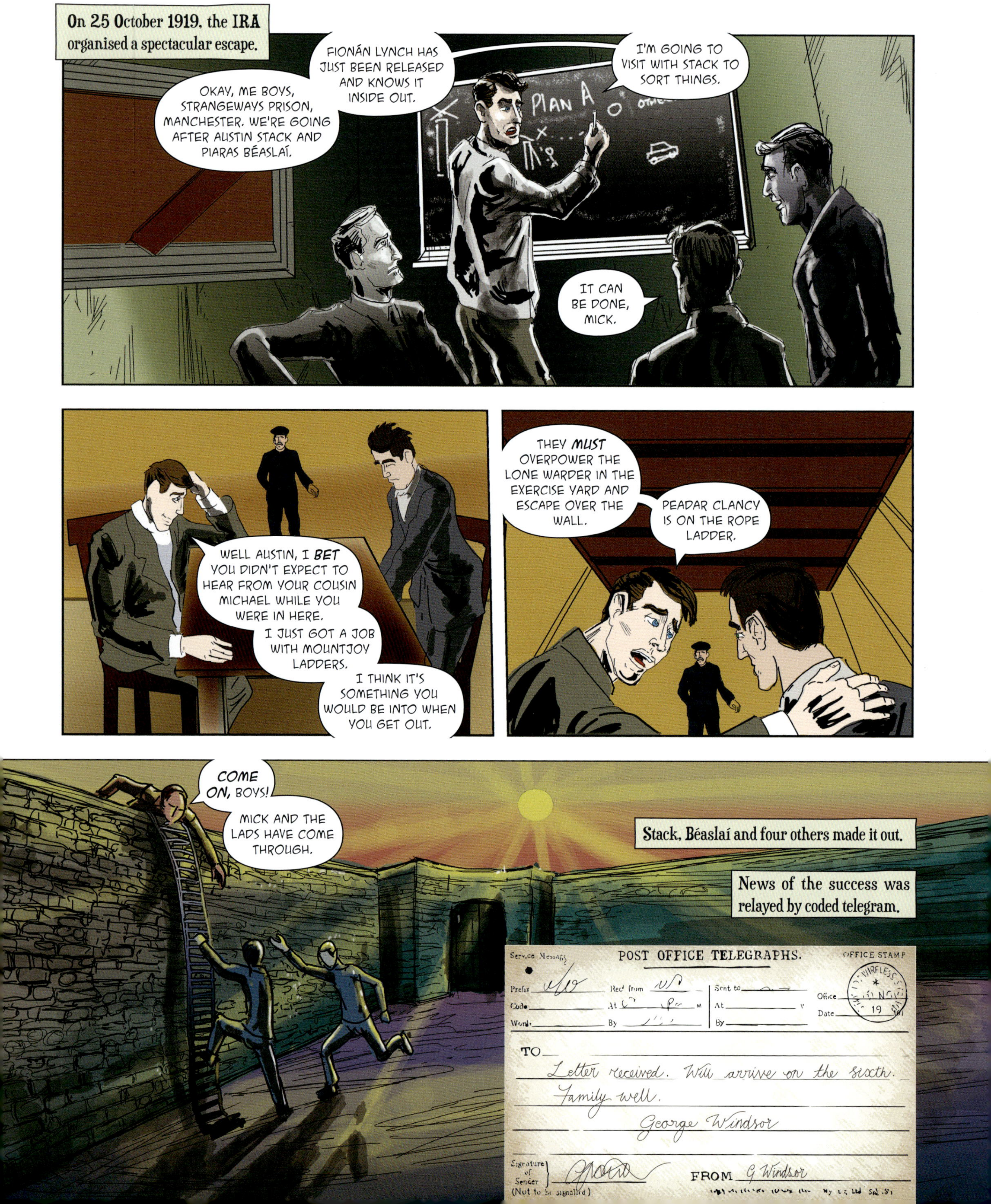

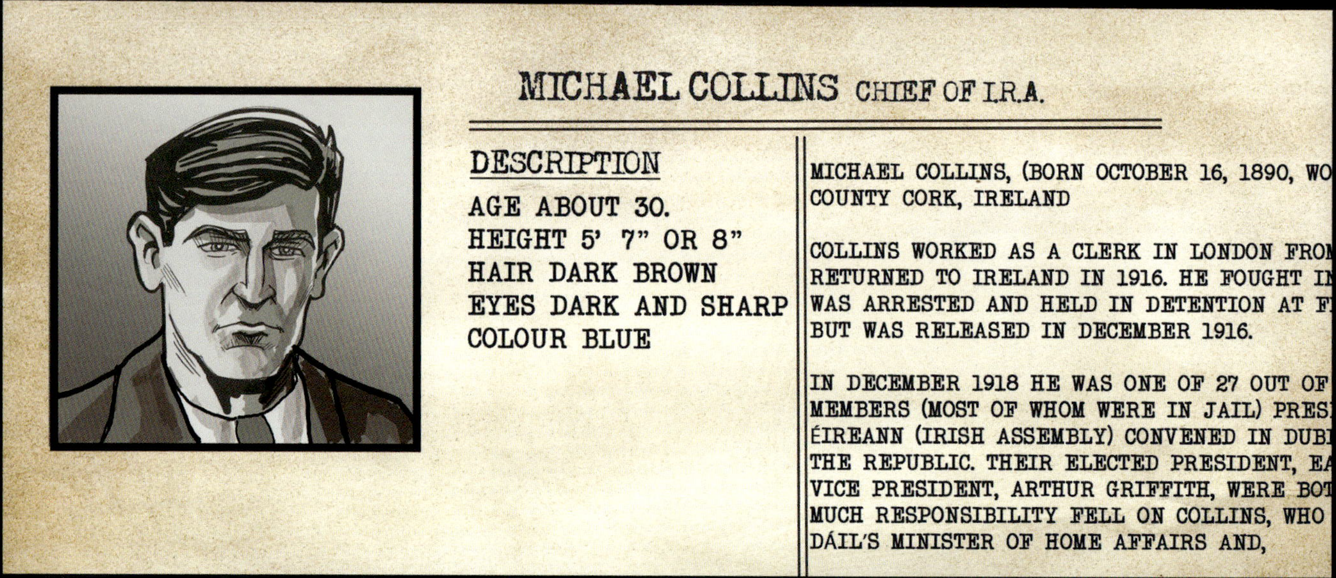

THE TWELVE APOSTLES, THE CAIRO GANG AND BLOODY SUNDAY

THE SQUAD

To counteract the brutality of the British authorities, Collins created a new special unit. Nicknamed the 'Squad' or the 'Twelve Apostles', its mission was to assassinate British agents and informers.

THE CAIRO GANG

The British brought in specialists trained in anti-insurgency to deal with this new threat. The 'Cairo Gang' were recruited from England, while the 'Igoe Gang' came from within Ireland.

Collins ordered the assassination of Viceroy Lord French, the English King's premier representative in Ireland. Lord French was hated for trying to introduce conscription.

Several attempts had been made to kill him. On 19 December 1919, he escaped once again. Young Volunteer Martin Savage was killed, and Dan Breen was injured.

21 January 1920, Harcourt Street. Paddy Daly, one of the leaders of the Squad, shot the new Police Assistant Commissioner, William Redmond.

"A BULLET-PROOF WAISTCOAT WON'T SAVE YOU FROM A SHOT TO THE HEAD!"

20 March 1920. Lord Mayor of Cork Tomás Mac Curtain was shot dead on his 36th birthday, in front of his family, by the Black and Tans, causing an international outcry. In August, RIC District Inspector Oswald Swanzy, who had ordered the attack, was killed with Mac Curtain's own revolver.

26 March 1920. Alan Bell, who searched bank accounts for Sinn Féin's National Loan, was dragged from a tram at Ballsbridge and shot dead.

The IRA brutally executed informers, putting them on display for others to learn a grim lesson.

A reward of £10,000 was offered for the capture or death of the Big Fella. Dublin city was locked down and military and police raids followed.

The Church condemned the outrages on all sides.

GOD SEES IT AS IT IS -- MURDER!!

PERPETRATORS WILL BE EXCOMMUNICATED.

LOTS OF CRITICISM OF THE TACTICS, MICK, THE CHURCH ESPECIALLY. THEY SEE US AS MURDERERS!

IS IT MURDER NOW TO FIGHT FOR THE FREEDOM OF YOUR COUNTRY? TELL IT TO TOM ASHE, OR TERENCE MCSWINEY!

12 August 1920. Terence MacSwiney, TD, Lord Mayor of Cork, was arrested. Deported to Brixton prison, he died on hunger strike on 25 October. His tri-coloured coffin was followed by thousands through London streets.

"GREATER LOVE THAN THIS NO MAN HATH, THAT A MAN LAY DOWN HIS LIFE FOR HIS FRIENDS."

IN LOVING MEMEORY OF
TERENCE MACSWINEY, TD
COMMANDANT 1ST BRIGADE I.R.A.
LORD MAYOR OF CORK

PRAY FOR THE SOUL OF A BOY WHO DIED FOR IRELAND
KEVIN GERALD BARRY
I.R.A.
EXECUTED IN
MOUNTJOY PRISON, DUBLIN

HANGED AT EIGHTEEN YEARS OLD. KEVIN BARRY, ANOTHER BLOODY MARTYR FOR DEAR OLD IRELAND. GOD REST YE!

AND NOW INTERNMENT CAMPS AT THE CURRAGH AND BALLYKINLAR, BUT SURE HUNDREDS ARE JOINING.

THEY CAN NEVER WIN THIS WAR.

Kevin Barry was executed on the 1 November for his part in an ambush which resulted in the deaths of three British soldiers.

MAY GOD HAVE MERCY ON YOUR SOULS.

On the morning of 21 November 1920, the Squad executed 13 British Secret Service agents as they lay in bed or were starting their day; another died later and four others were wounded. Terrified spies and their families banged on the gates of Dublin Castle seeking refuge. A concerted, well-planned, audacious and terrible act.

In August, de Valera, President of the Irish Republic, indicated they would be prepared to negotiate a treaty. He refused to attend talks himself, insisting Collins take his place.

"I AM A SOLDIER, NOT A POLITICIAN, BUT I WILL DO IT IN THE SPIRIT OF A SOLDIER OBEYING ORDERS. LET THEM MAKE A SCAPEGOAT OR WHATEVER THEY LIKE OF ME. SOMEONE MUST GO"

The Irish negotiating team were Arthur Griffith, Michael Collins, Robert Barton, Eamonn Duggan and Erskine Childers. They also had a secretarial team, as well as bodyguards and an intelligence contingent, comprised of Ned Broy, Emmet Dalton, Liam Tobin, Tom Cullen and Joseph Dolan of the Squad.

The British negotiators included Prime Minister David Lloyd George, Colonial Secretary Winston Churchill and Lord Chancellor Baron Birkenhead. Unionists refused to attend the peace talks.

Lloyd George quickly demanded a signature or 'immediate and terrible war'.

"I MAY HAVE SIGNED MY DEATH WARRANT."

The Anglo-Irish Treaty was signed on 6 December 1921. It gave dominion status to the Irish Free State.

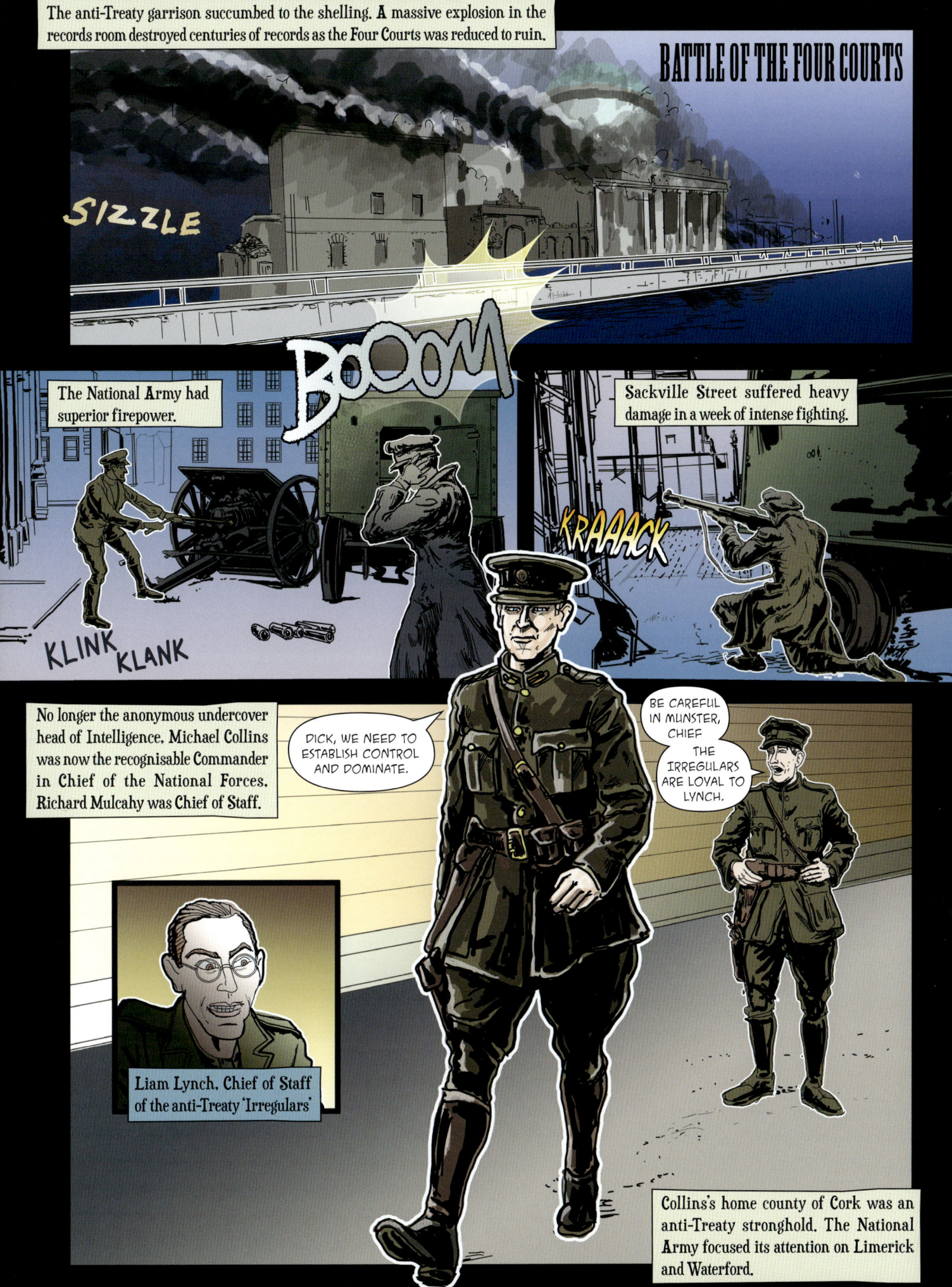

20 August 1922. Mick and Fionán Lynch set off for Cork. They stopped at Maryborough (Portlaoise) Prison, Roscrea Barracks and Limerick, meeting with General Eoin O'Duffy.

Maryborough Prison

Their little convoy moved on to Mallow and Cork and the Imperial Hotel, banging the heads together of 2 sentries he found asleep.

He met with Major General Emmet Dalton and with businesspeople, consulted about stolen National Loan funds and had dinner with his sister.

DELICIOUS, MARY.

21 August. Mick and Emmet Dalton inspected military posts and banks in the city and in Macroom. The convoy was surrounded by curious soldiers and civilians. They took a drink at a hotel bar.

The convoy returned to Cork, where Mick dined again with his sister Mary and other relatives. Then more meetings, with politicians, military men and businesspeople.

The convoy included a motorcyclist and a Crossley tender full of soldiers, with a mounted Lewis gun. Collins and Dalton rode in a yellow Leland touring car with a driver and reserve driver. There was also an armoured car, the Sliabh na mBan, with a Vickers machine gun.

From Macroom they set out for Bantry, via Bandon. The convoy asked a man called Dinny Long for directions at a crossroads at Béal na mBláth.

"CAN YOU TELL US THE BEST WAY TO GET TO BANDON?"

"YOU WOULD BE BEST GOING THROUGH NEWCESTON — THERE HAVE BEEN ROADBLOCKS LATELY."

"GOOD MAN. DRIVE ON."

Dinny Long ran to a house nearby, where officers of the local anti-Treaty IRA Brigade under Tom Hales were to meet. Long was a sentry outside the meeting; he had just laid down his rifle to take a short walk when the convoy came along.

It was decided to ambush the convoy on its return. The road was barricaded and mined with explosives.

Mick met with Commandant Seán Hales in Bandon. As they left Lee's Hotel, the last known photo was taken of Mick, with Dalton in the rear seat of the car.

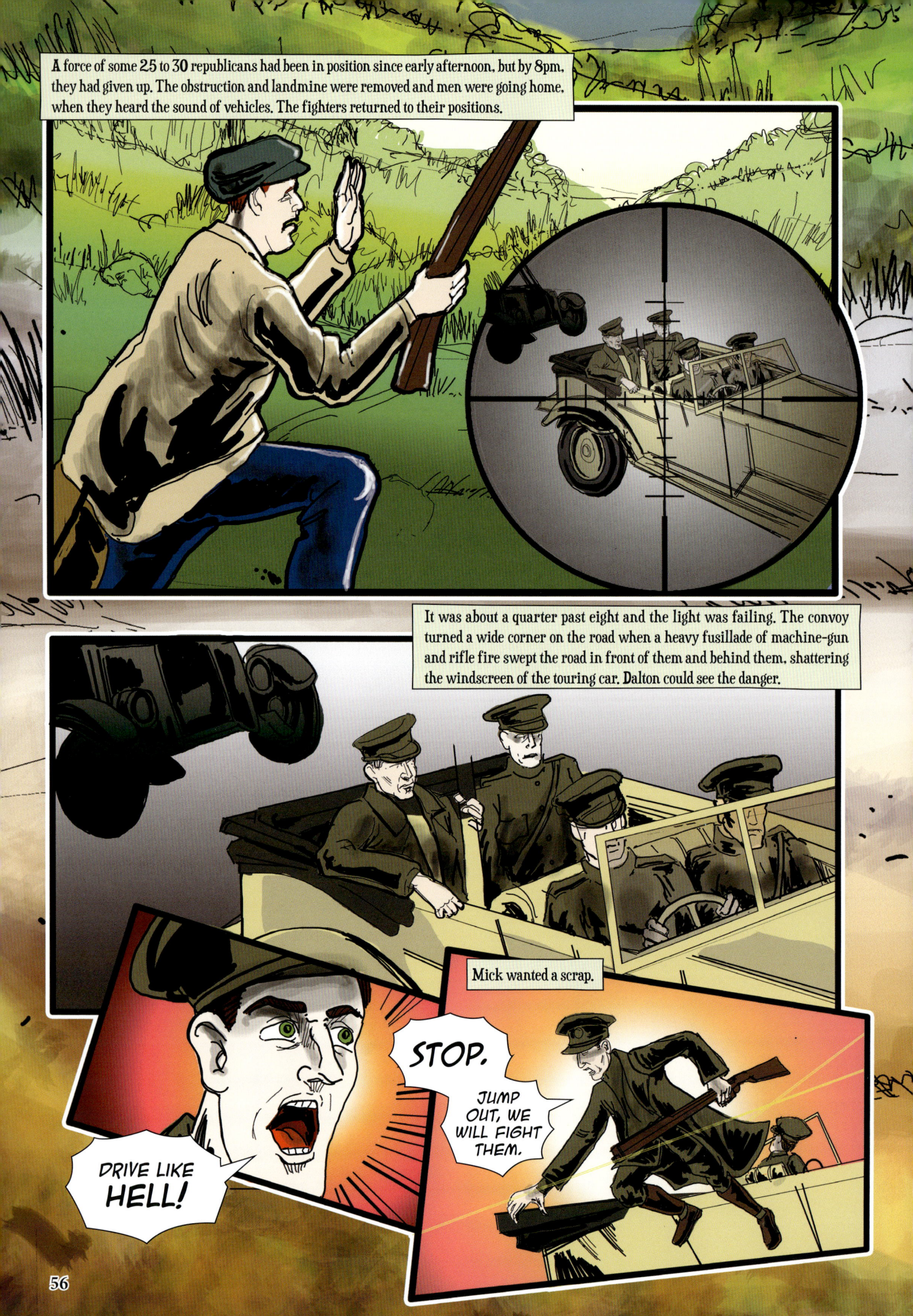

Men spread out and took cover where they could. The armoured car's machine gun opened fire. The machine-gunners and riflemen dismounted from the Crossley tender and began firing. After about twenty minutes, without casualties, there was a lull in the fighting. Collins jumped to his feet, firing occasional shots, using the armoured car as cover.

PING
DEHDEHDEH
WHHRRRR
PING

THERE THEY ARE RUNNING UP THE ROAD!

COME ON, BOYS!

KRAKK

Mick moved away from the armoured car and cover, taking a firing position in the middle of the road. Dalton and the others could hear him firing away.

DEHDEHDEH
WHHRRRR
BANG
PING

The machine gun jammed in the turret of the Sliabh na mBan, followed by a few moments of silence.

Seán his elder brother said a tearful last goodbye.

The funeral mass took place at Dublin's Pro-Cathedral, and some 500,000 people lined the streets as his body made its last journey to Glasnevin Cemetery at the head of a 3-mile funeral procession.

GO MALL MÁIRSEÁIL

The only floral tribute permitted on the coffin was a single white lily from Kitty Kiernan. Kitty wept for Ireland and her true love; her fiancé. She was inconsolable.

MICHAEL COLLINS GAVE HIS LIFE FOR HIS COUNTRY ...

And yet he may have baulked at all of the pomp and ceremony. If the British had got him, he would have demanded a funeral to stop the world, but he had been killed by his own countrymen in the country he had loved to call his own.

Gearóid Ó Súilleabháin and Michael Collins were not only comrades and friends from west Cork, they were engaged to be married to the Kiernan sisters, Maud and Kitty, in a double wedding in November 1922. Gearóid and Maud did marry, and Kitty attended, dressed in mourning black.